Fun Runs

By Heather Hammonds

Contents

Fun Runs for Everyone

Fun runs are races.
People run from the starting line
to the finishing line
in fun runs.

People who cannot run
can walk or ride in fun runs.

Some fun runs are held
at the same time every year.
Thousands of people run in them.

People run in fun runs by themselves,
or with friends.
Sometimes, teams of people
enter fun runs together.

Some schools hold fun runs.
Children run around the school grounds,
or a sports oval.

Sometimes, teams from different schools enter fun runs.
Each team tries to win for their school.

Sometimes, people enter fun runs
to raise money.
People pay to run in the fun run.
Then, the money is given
to people in need.

At the end of many fun runs,
the runners are given something
to drink and eat.
Those people who come first
may get a prize, too!

How to Hold a School Fun Run

Goal

To hold a school fun run.

Materials

You will need:

- teachers to help

- pencils

- paper

- a map of the fun run course

- certificates for everyone in the fun run

- ribbons for the winners in each class

- water

- fruit for everyone to eat after the fun run.

Before the Fun Run

Steps

1. Make a map of the fun run course, with your teacher's help.

2. Design a certificate.

3. Ask your teacher to make copies of the map and the certificate for everyone in the race.

4. Train hard for many days before the fun run.

5. Invite your parents, grandparents, and other people in your family to come and watch the fun run.

On the Day of the Fun Run

6. Do warm-up exercises before the race.

7. Line up and wait for a teacher to start the race.

8. Run or walk around the course.

9. Drink some water and eat some fruit,
   after the race is over.

10. Cheer the winners
    as they get their ribbons.

11. Thank the teacher
    as you get your certificate.